Instagram Marketing

A Comprehensive Guide to Growing Your Brand on Instagram

Table of Contents

Introduction 1

Chapter One: What is Instagram Marketing? 3

Chapter Two: Instagram to Grow Your Business 8

Chapter Three: Strategies to Grow Your Instagram Audience . 30

Chapter Four: Instagram Ads 39

Chapter Five: Influencer Marketing 63

Conclusion 78

Introduction

Social media has taken the world by storm in the last two decades, and it is here to stay. Safe to say, Instagram is probably one of the most widely used and successful social media platforms in the world. There are nearly 1-billion users actively using this platform, and it is only second to Facebook. The point is, you have the opportunity to reach all these people if you use Instagram the right way.

Instagram has a simple and user-friendly interface that makes it accessible for just about everyone. It is not just a platform for sharing photos and videos with your friends and family anymore. Every business with an up-to-date marketing strategy now has an online presence on Instagram. This has happened because they recognize the immense value of the large user base signed up on it already. And it has been working effectively for many brands. Another advantage is that Instagram has consistently been working on updating its features to make it a lot more functional for marketers. Now the only question is whether you will be able to make it work for yourself as well.

In the following chapters, you will be learning about a variety of marketing strategies and will gain access to a lot of tips that will help you leverage Instagram in the best way possible. If you want to use Instagram for marketing, you need to take a step-by-step approach. Once you are finished reading this simple guide, you will know exactly what steps to take to begin marketing your business on Instagram successfully.

Chapter One: What is Instagram Marketing?

So, you want to learn about Instagram marketing and successfully grow your brand through Instagram. Before you start setting up ad campaigns or reaching out to influencers, you need to know the basics.

Instagram marketing falls under social media marketing and focuses on using Instagram to promote a business. This has a broad scope since Instagram marketing can accomplish different kinds of goals using various strategies or tactics.

Instagram marketing can be done in two different ways:

- Through paid tactics such as Instagram Ads, Promoted Posts, or Influencer Marketing

- Through unpaid tactics where the brand is grown organically through content like Instagram stories, posts, etc.

Typically, the goals of a business investing in Instagram marketing include sales, a bigger following, higher engagement, and increased brand awareness.

Instagram has its own algorithm that determines what users will see in their feed. The term *'algorithm'* itself is quite misunderstood. You don't need to understand every little detail of how the Instagram algorithm works for you to make it work in your favor. You just need to understand the basics of it to use it to achieve your goals from Instagram marketing. The algorithm is explained in more detail in the next chapter of this guide.

There are many marketers and even users who feel that the Instagram algorithm is their enemy. This is the opposite of what the algorithm is meant for. The ultimate goal of this algorithm is to give users an optimized experience on the platform. It aims to show users entertaining, relevant, and engaging content for them individually. User activity and behavior are studied to decide what they might want to view on their feed in the future. The main takeaway from this is that you should create content that will interest and benefit the audience you want to target.

Examples of Instagram Marketing

Organic Content

This is an umbrella term that includes any content that you post without paying for it. It could be videos, photos, or even Stories that are not paid for. It is important to create organic content consistently for your Instagram marketing campaign.

Instagram Ads

A more direct approach to Instagram marketing involves Instagram Ads. This paid-for content will help to generate cold, hard sales for your brand. Instagram Ads can be of different types and include Story ads, video ads, image ads, etc. Instagram Ads are explained in detail later in this guide since they are a crucial component of Instagram marketing.

Influencer Marketing

Influencer marketing is an extremely popular way of marketing on Instagram these days. Influencers are people who have organically grown their following on Instagram through their content. Influencers can belong to any industry and usually focus on one niche. Influencers are present on most social media platforms and could specialize in specific content on anything from tech to fashion.

Brands need to look for influencers from their industry to market the brand through them successfully. Influencer marketing helps to generate a serious amount of engagement, more followers, and overall brand awareness. The key to influencer marketing is finding the most suitable influencers for the brand. If you are a food brand, you should find an influencer in the food industry that can create food-based content that appeals to their followers.

Here is a basic idea for an Instagram marketing strategy for your brand:

1. Set goals for your presence on Instagram. What do you want to achieve from it?

2. Determine the target audience you want to reach through your Instagram account and marketing efforts.

3. Do competitive analysis. Figure out what is working for other businesses like yours on Instagram. Collect data about your target audience.

4. Create a schedule for all your posts and ads. Consistency is key to beat the Instagram algorithm and to grow your following.

5. Build your brand on Instagram.

6. Work on growing your follower count through organic as well as paid channels.

7. Convert the followers from Instagram into real customers for your business.

As you read this guide, you will learn how to do all this and more once you open a business account on Instagram. Strategy plays an important role in social media marketing, and it is not just about creating an account on every platform possible. If you want to use Instagram to your advantage, make sure you truly focus on it. This platform performs best for businesses that are consistently active on it. Instagram is also quite different from most other social media websites and will require a different approach. If you put in the time and effort, the rewards you can see from Instagram marketing are well worth it!

Chapter Two: Instagram to Grow Your Business

Instagram can be used for growing your business and establishing yourself solidly in your industry. There are many ways in which you can do this with Instagram marketing.

If you want to use Instagram for business, the first thing to do is create a presence on Instagram for your brand.

Create an Account

The first step towards success on Instagram is obviously to create an account for your brand on the platform. It is as simple as downloading the application on your device and using your email id or phone number to sign up. It is available for both Android and iOS devices. Create a unique username that will make it easy for users to search for you and remember your account. Set a secure password, and you're done. With these simple steps, your brand now has a presence on Instagram.

Switch from Personal to a Business Account

Since you will be using this account for building your brand, opt for the business account option. On your profile, go to Settings and click on Account. You will see the choice for "Switch to a professional account." Tap on the Business option and follow the prompts. Using this business account option allows you to utilize Instagram features that are built especially for businesses. When your account is on the Personal account mode, you can choose to keep it Private. This means that people will only see your posts if you accept their follow request. Business accounts are automatically on Public mode, which means that anyone on Instagram can view your posts. It is important to be on Public mode, so your posts have a chance to show up on the Instagram Explore page. This will allow you to reach more users with your content.

Instagram Business Account Features

Instagram Shopping

This update is relatively new and allows business accounts to add direct links to their products by tagging their posts. If you post a picture with a certain outfit, the clothes can be tagged with a link that will lead the user to the product page. They don't have to search for products on websites anymore. It is a very convenient way for people to shop for things they see on Instagram. Instagram Checkout is slowly being rolled out in most countries. This gives users the opportunity to complete their entire purchase process on Instagram itself instead of being directed to another site.

Instagram Ads

The advertising tools on Instagram are the same as those on Facebook. You can use these to set up ad campaigns for your brand on Instagram, and track their performance using a variety of metrics. You will learn more about Instagram ads later in the book.

Instagram Insights

For any business, it is important to pay attention to analytics. When you switch to the business account mode on Instagram, you get access to Instagram analytics. This gives you information on profile views, website clicks, email clicks, reach, impressions, and more. All of this gives you an idea about how your posts are performing on Instagram. You also get demographic data about your followers' ages, gender, activity peak, and location. All the insight you get from this feature will be valuable in brand growth. It will help you understand how every post performs and will also aid in improving your marketing strategy.

Quick Replies and Primary and General Messaging Inboxes

The Quick Replies feature allows you to set up instant replies to messages from your followers. This makes it quite easy for you to respond to all the messages flooding into your inbox. You can also sort your messages into two folders - primary and general.

Call to Action Button and Contact Options

On a business account, you have "Contact" buttons on your profile. You can add a location, phone number, and address for your business. This makes it easy for followers to contact you with this information. You also have access to Action buttons like Reserve, Gift Cards, and Order Food. A lot of small businesses have benefited from these features on the app.

Promote Posts

Instagram also gives you the opportunity to promote your posts. A promoted post is featured on the feeds of the audience you target. As you will see later in this book, it is rather easy to set up such promoted posts.

Links for Instagram Stories

Once your account has more than 10k followers, you can add links directly to your Instagram Stories. Your followers just have to swipe up on the story to reach the link you have added. This gives you a direct route for generating sales and more brand engagement.

Grow Your Business with Instagram

Use the following pointers to grow your business with Instagram:

Define Your Goals

Instagram is only a tool for your business. To use it well, you need to know what you want to use it for. Setting clear goals is crucial. What do you want to use your Instagram profile for? Is it for increasing brand awareness? Do you want to get new leads? Is it for creating an online presence for your brand? Do you want to sell your products directly through Instagram? It could be any or all of these. But you have to know what the goal for your Instagram marketing strategy is if you want to achieve it.

Define Your Audience

Although you have access to millions of users on the platform, you need to know your target audience. Defining your target market will help you create content and a marketing strategy that is tailored for them. The more specific you are, the easier it becomes to target the right audience. You can research to figure out the age range, gender, location, etc., for the target audience. You can then create your content according to that audience. This information is particularly important when you want to set up Instagram ads, since you can then target that demographic specifically.

Optimize Your Bio

You get 150 characters for your Instagram bio, and you should try your best to make every one of them count. Your bio gives you the chance to make a good first impression on anyone first viewing your profile. Try to convey your brand personality as best as possible and convince them to follow your profile. It might seem like a tough ask, but it can be done. Do research on other brands in your niche that have a good following on Instagram and get ideas for writing your bio.

Your Profile Photo

As a business, you have the option to use your brand logo as your profile photo. This is the best way to have people recognize your business at a glance.

Visually Compelling Content

Instagram is all about visuals, and your posts have to be attractive to anyone viewing them. You don't need to hire professional photographers or buy extremely expensive equipment, however. You simply need to make sure that the photos or videos you upload are well lit, clear, and well-composed. These days, most smartphones have great cameras and editing features or apps to help you achieve an aesthetic Instagram feed. Even if you don't upload photos and instead use infographics or animations, they should have high clarity and be eye-catching. Any visual content you upload on Instagram should be compelling. When your photos tell a story, your audience can connect better with the brand. The content has to be engaging for viewers.

Here are several ideas for great engaging content:

- **Behind the Scenes Posts:** Post images or videos about what happens behind the scenes at your business. It could be pictures of your office or a story of someone working on a product. This gives the user a more personal experience with the brand through Instagram.

- **Regrams and User-Generated Content:** Share or upload pictures or videos that users have created with your products. This is always compelling and encourages other users to create content around your brand.

• **Videos:** You can upload a video of up to 60 seconds on your feed, or an even longer video on IGTV. This is a great way to share content with users and elaborate on any story you want to relay through a marketing campaign.

• **Reels:** This new feature is another great way to share videos in a multi-cut format.

• **Quotes or Other Text-Based Images:** You can create interesting text-based content for your feed as well.

• **Instructional Posts:** You can use the platform to share posts on how your products can be used in different ways. For instance, if you have a furniture business, you can create videos showing the furniture being set up in an aesthetic space.

When you create compelling content, users will be inspired to share it on their own feed or through messages. This will help you reach an even wider audience for your brand. When you create content, focus on creating something visually appealing that compels users to share it with others.

Create Your Brand

When you plan the content for your brand, you should think of how the posts will look on your feed. When someone clicks on your username and is directed to your profile, you get the chance to make a quick impression. If they like what they see, there's a good chance that they will follow you.

If you have too much random content and no proper aesthetic, it is harder to catch their attention. Color has a big impact on users and will affect brand recognition and buying decisions. Maintaining a consistent aesthetic across your posts will help users recognize your content more easily when it appears on their feed. One easy way to achieve this is by using the same filter or preset for all your posts. Instagram has its own filters that are great, but you can also use apps like Lightroom to try other effects or create your own presets for your account. Many creators sell their presets on Lightroom as well. If you like someone's feed, you can check if they are selling their presets or have shared any information on how they edit their images.

Make Your Caption Count

Instagram is a very visual platform, but you should not neglect the captions for your posts. The brand voice has to go hand in hand with the brand look. You can add captions with a limit of

2200 characters. This means you can add a detailed story below your post or just a catchy short one. The first two caption lines are what appear to the user without them having to click on the "more" option, so you need to have a great start if you want them to read the rest. Any important information should be included in those first two lines since statistically speaking, most users don't read the rest. The recommended characters for captions on organic posts are 140-150, and for Instagram Ads are 125. You can always write a longer caption if you have a compelling story to share. Your caption should always be relevant to the post, entertaining, and on-brand.

Use Hashtags Wisely

Hashtags will help to make your brand and posts more visible and discoverable. Each post is allowed a maximum of 30 hashtags, but this is not a cue to add that many on every post. If users see 30 hashtags under each post, they might view it as spam. It is even worse if none of those hashtags are relevant to your brand or the post. Always use hashtags that are specific to your niche and relevant. Don't use hashtags that encourage like or follow swapping.

Engage

If you want more engagement on your Instagram account, you have to be engaging as well. Your content is important, but you should not forget about the post after you upload it. Go back and reply to any comments or messages left by users. Interact with them on their profiles as well and create a connection. The minimum requirement for engagement is to reply to a comment on your posts. You should also find other accounts that belong to your niche and follow them or engage with comments and likes. This will make your account more visible in an organic way. Those accounts will appreciate your effort, and their users will notice your comments and be directed to your profile. When someone tags you in their post, leave a like or a comment. If the aesthetic fits your account, you can even repost it on your feed but, if not, you could share it in your stories. When you go through your posts' comments, pin the ones by your top fans at the top. You could also pin any comments that look interesting or may encourage conversations among other users. Engaging with others will increase the engagement rate on your account.

Post on Instagram Stories

Most businesses use Instagram stories quite actively these days. They have also reported great results from using this feature for marketing. According to statistics, a third of the most-viewed stories on Instagram are from businesses. This is why stories are now an important part of Instagram marketing strategies.

Since stories will disappear after 24 hours, you don't have to be as particular about them as you are about the posts on your feed. Users prefer something more raw and fun on stories. You can use them to connect with users through features like Polls. Stories can be used for telling a story, providing valuable information to followers, or prompt action through the "Swipe Up" feature. You can also use them for building consistent brand identity by engaging with users. You should also try to re-share stories that other users tag you in.

Boost Your Profile Section with Highlighted Stories and Covers

Another recent feature of Instagram is the highlights component. You can now create albums of highlights from your archived stories. This will allow your top content to be viewable by users even after 24 hours have passed. These albums are visible right below the general bio section. You can make them more attractive or in sync with the rest of your profile by creating custom covers for the albums. You could simply use the best story as your cover as well. Add a label to inform users about what the album contains. For instance, a fashion influencer may have albums labeled as Outfits, Makeup, Shoes, etc. This allows users to know what they can expect when they click on the album. If your business sells products, you could create albums for each category.

Use the Countdown Sticker for Product Launches or Events

The countdown sticker on Stories is a very interactive feature. You can use it to build up anticipation for any upcoming event or product launch. It will provide your followers with an alert for the event if they select the option to mark their calendar. It's a tool that many brands use for announcing events like sales or contests. The sticker also gives top followers the chance to get real-time updates and gain access to offers before others. It is a great way for brands to make sure that their products get many orders as soon as they are launched.

Go Live

The Instagram Live feature is another one brands should utilize to connect with their audience. It has great potential since it allows real-time communication with fans from all over the world. You can use the countdown sticker to announce the schedule for a live session. This is something a lot of celebrities and influencers do before a live session. You can even invest in influencer marketing and allow an influencer to take over your stories and hold a live session as part of a campaign. This will direct a lot of traffic from the influencers following to your own profile, along with encourage engagement from your existing followers. This feature can also be used for sharing a real-time event or behind-the-scenes actions. Many brands use the Live feature to share tutorials or host workshops. This could be an interview with team members or other interesting people. It could also be a question-and-answer session where users get to ask questions about the brand and its products or services.

Set Up a Shop on Instagram

Instagram Shops are yet another new feature that is extremely beneficial for businesses. This feature can only be used by accounts that have a business profile. Brands can open their online store directly on Instagram with this. It also adds a "View Shop" button on your profile page. Fans can tap on this tab and browse through your shop without having to view one post at a time. The Explore Page also has a Shop tab now, and users are shown new products that they might be interested in. Millions of users have been using this feature to shop from Instagram, and it is a great opportunity for Instagram marketers to tap into. Shopping products can be tagged on stories, posts, and IGTV.

Create Instagram Reels

The Reels tab is another feature to tap into. These are similar to TikTok videos but can be used for much more than dance clips. Brands have been using Reels to make their content more visible since there is lesser competition on it right now. Reels can be used for organic as well as paid content.

Post at the Right Time

Timing matters, and analytics will give you a good idea about when you should be posting. There is no perfect timing that every brand uses. It varies from business to business and depends on factors like location. Insights will tell you the times at which users are more active on your profile each day. You can then use this to choose the perfect time to reach the maximum number of users when you post. The first couple of hours within which you post are crucial for higher engagement. Posting at the wrong time might prevent your post from being viewed by a lot of your audience, so be very mindful about this!

Use Instagram Ads to Expand Your Audience

The easiest way to get your content in front of more people is through Instagram ads. When you have defined a target audience for your brand, you can use these demographics to target users for your ads as well. Instagram advertising is explained in detail later in the book.

Use Analytics to Refine Your Marketing Strategy

Your Instagram marketing strategy might be doing well, but it can always do better. You can use Insights and other analytical tools to learn a lot from any past or running campaigns. This data can then be used to improve your marketing efforts in the future and optimize your content.

Understand the Instagram Algorithm

Instagram marketing cannot work if you don't understand the Instagram algorithm. This elusive algorithm plays a big role in how well a post does on Instagram. In recent years, you might have noticed that the Instagram feed doesn't work the same way as it did before. Many people are still trying to figure out why their engagement is so low and how they can start reaching more people. Fortunately for you, this guide will help you learn enough about this algorithm to survive it.

According to Instagram, their algorithm does not hide your posts, and it only personalizes user feeds according to how they use the platform. The posts or accounts that you engage with, and the frequency with which you use the app; are what decide what shows up on your feed first, and this is how it will work for your followers as well.

Instagram Algorithm Key Factors

Timeliness

The algorithm considers the time at which you post something as well. This is because they want users to see the latest and most engaging posts. By studying the data from Insights, you can figure out the best time for posting. This will help you surpass the algorithm and get more likes and engagement on a post. You should post at a time when more of your followers are active. If you post when your followers are inactive, your post gets pushed down on their feed, and they will see other recent posts instead.

Frequency

The more frequently you use the app, the more chronological your feed will look. This is because the algorithm tries to show you the most recent content. The less often you check the app, the less chronological it will be. At this point, the algorithm will consider what posts you engage with more often while determining the order of posts on your feed.

Interest

Instagram takes the interests of the user into account while determining what should be shown on their feed. It is not just about whom you follow, but also the type of posts you have liked or searched for in the past. When the algorithm thinks that you are more likely to "like" a certain type of post, it will push it up on your feed. Your Instagram behavior is what determines what you see in your feed. The posts you comment on or like more often, accounts you interact with, and those you tag or whose posts you are tagged in will be all factor in. If you want your posts to be pushed up by the algorithm, you should be consistently active on the platform. This will give your audience a better chance to see your content on their feed. This doesn't mean that you have to be on your phone constantly. Use apps such as Later to schedule your posting schedule and set aside time to interact with other accounts. Engagement is important for the algorithm, and this includes likes, comments, reposts, and views. All of these factors will help you to beat the algorithm.

Usage

The more time you spend on Instagram, the more posts you see. When you spend a lot of time on the app, you might even see that you keep seeing the same posts on your feed. This is when Instagram will show you posts from accounts that you don't follow as suggestions. The less time you spend, the more specific the content on your feed will be.

Relationship

The algorithm also tries to give priority to posts from accounts that you have a better relationship with. This is why posts from your friends, family, or any account you interact with will appear first on your feed. The algorithm will calculate your relationship by following how you engage with someone's content by liking or commenting, or by how often you search for them or send them messages. This is why it's vital to build relationships with your users and engage often with them.

Who You Follow

When you follow many people from your account, the algorithm has more posts to choose from. This makes it hard for you to see posts from everyone. When you follow fewer accounts, you are more likely to be up to date with all their posts. It would be better to stop following inactive accounts or any ghost followers.

The Instagram algorithm works similarly for the Explore page as well as your personal feed. It will show you the content that it thinks you will be most interested in and engage with. This will be determined by the interactions you have had in the past with different accounts. Similarly, when you engage with users, you will be more likely to show up on their feed if they follow you, or on their Explore page if they don't. The Explore page is always evolving as Instagram rolls out new features and functionalities. It is not hard to get your posts on the Explore page. The algorithm will always try its best to serve users with content that is best suited for them. If you upload content with catchy captions and relevant hashtags, it will use this information to show your posts to the right audience.

Here are a few ways in which you can improve your ranking on the Instagram algorithm:

> 1. Use the latest features rolled out by Instagram. When Instagram rolls out a new feature, the algorithm pushes content created with those features. They do this to promote the feature and encourage more people to adopt it. For instance, when the IGTV option was added, the algorithm pushed all the content created with it

regardless of how popular those accounts originally were. This gave a lot of people a chance to gain more followers. If you see a new feature on Instagram, use it and upload content.

2. Use engaging captions and comment more often to drive conversations. Instagram has said that they give importance to posts that have a lot of comment engagement. This means that you should try to encourage people to comment more often on your posts. To do this, you need engaging captions. You should always include a call-to-action on your caption, or at least as often as possible. It could be a question, or you could ask them to share their opinion on something, or just ask them to tag a friend.

3. Use stickers on Instagram Stories to encourage interactions. The best stickers to boost engagement are the question, poll, and emoji slider stickers. These are a quick and easy way for people to interact with your account. You can even use these stickers to research for your business since it allows you to gain information on what your followers want or would like to see from your business.

It is up to you to figure out the best way to improve your business's algorithm ranking. Use analytics to understand how your followers can be engaged with the best, and don't hesitate to try out new Instagram features when they are first made available. Engage regularly with your followers and encourage them to interact with you through comments, polls, and questions on your stories.

Chapter Three: Strategies to Grow Your Instagram Audience

It's all about building your audience on Instagram. The more followers you have, the larger the audience you reach and the more potential customers you have for your business. This is why it is crucial to implement strategies that will help you organically grow your Instagram following.

The term '*organic*' is important here because many people and businesses resort to buying followers or paying for more likes on their posts. It may seem like an easy hack to pay a little money for more followers/likes, but does it really help you? The answer is a clear no. Most of these followers or likes will be from ghost accounts or bots. You won't be generating any new leads for your business. Your content will not be reaching the audience that you want to be targeting. Inorganic growth will just give you a higher number on your following and like count. But these numbers will have no value.

When you do it the right way and focus on organic growth instead, you will see a slow but steady growth that is meaningful. You cannot assume that your follower count will start growing just because you have an account and start posting content. The app has gone through many changes in the last decade, and it is constantly being worked on. With every tweak the Instagram team makes, you have to make changes to your own Instagram strategy. It is important to understand the ins and outs of how the app works and adapts. With that said, there are several proven growth strategies that you can try for your business to solidify your brand presence online.

Instagram growth is usually just seen as an increase in the number of followers. But you have to work on brand exposure, account engagement, and better content to gain these followers increase. Why would people follow your account if you don't engage them with content that appeals to them? Once you start posting, you can use Instagram Insights to understand what your audience likes. You can then use this data to grow your business further. Don't opt for any services that give you fake followers and likes in exchange for payments. It will harm your business and may even result in your account getting banned from the platform.

Growth Strategies

Consistency

Consistency is key when it comes to Instagram. This is one of the basic things that you have to remember. You should post content frequently and keep your audience engaged. This doesn't mean that you have to post multiple times a day or even every day. But you can't post every day for a month and suddenly go off-grid for the next month. Uploading at least 4-5 times a week is ideal. You can even post once every day if you have engaging content ready. You can't depend on a single post to go viral and make your account popular in one go. You have to create content and post at a frequency that allows you to reach your targeted audience at their most active timing. You can check your analytics to figure out a posting schedule for your account. Posting at the right time and with consistency is important if you want higher engagement. When you have a consistent posting schedule, your audience will know when they can look forward to your next post. You should make sure that you don't compromise on content quality just to keep up with your posting schedule. There is a lot of content consistently being uploaded on Instagram, and you need to stand out if you want more followers. If you post sub-par content, your current followers might choose to unfollow you, too.

Run Contests and Promotions

The fact is everyone loves a free gift or discount. This is something that won't change and applies to people of all demographics. As a marketer, it is important to post and offer things that consumers really want. You don't have to keep offering discounts or free gifts and run your business into the ground. Even if you offer a promotion or discount a couple of times a year, people will look forward to it. You have to figure out what you can afford and what will advance your business. When you post content with discount codes or promotions, it catches the consumer's eye and encourages them to follow you so they can stay updated with any future offers. Running a contest is also a great way to surge your follower count. The contest can have rules like "Tag 3 friends and make them follow the account" or "Repost this on your account." Most people are willing to follow such call-to-action in exchange for a chance of winning a prize. If you run a contest or offer a promotion once a month or even every three months, your followers will likely stick around for the next one.

Focus on Good Content

Content is king. What you post on your account will make all the difference. Depending on the kind of business you run or the type of branding you want to do, create relative and engaging content. Invest time and, if required, money on content. It is not just about your in-feed posts on Instagram anymore. Instagram now allows you to upload IGTV videos, Reels, and Stories. You should diversify the content you produce as much as possible so you can utilize every feature on the platform and engage users consistently. Even if you don't have great content to post on your feed, stay engaged with users by uploading Instagram Stories. These don't require much effort and can be a fun way to connect. Share what is happening behind the scenes or just about anything you want on your Stories. There are a lot of fun filters that you can use to make your stories engaging as well. You also can create and upload your own filter on the app and make it accessible to users. You can create gifs or stickers for your business, too, and encourage followers to use these on their own Instagram Stories. There are many ways in which you can use Stories to engage users. Check out popular accounts in the same industry as yours and see what kind of content is performing best for them.

Cross-Platform Promotion

Social media platforms are all useful in their own way. Don't stick solely to Instagram, and instead, create a presence on the major platforms that your business can benefit from. Create and post content on each of these platforms, then leverage the following of each to increase your following on Instagram as well. Most people, as well as businesses, have multiple accounts on social media. Instagram, Facebook, Twitter, and Pinterest are a few of the main ones you might choose to focus on. Every platform has its own strength, and you should try to create content with that specific platform in mind. You can offer promotions or contests on other platforms as a way to encourage users to follow your Instagram account. On a platform like Pinterest, it is easy to gain more exposure for your visual content. You can post your Instagram content on Pinterest and direct users to your Instagram account. It is also easier to gain views on a single post on Pinterest for a longer time than on Instagram.

You can also promote your Instagram account on other digital spaces. It is not necessary to stick solely to social media. Send out newsletters or upload digital ads that include a link to your Instagram account.

If you have a physical store or office, you can encourage customers to follow your Instagram account in exchange for a small discount. Add a QR code on your packaging or bills to help customers find your account quickly.

Cross-platform promotions help you bring customers from other platforms to your Instagram and is an easy way to increase follower count.

Increase Engagement

Higher engagement with followers and potential customers will help you build a relationship with them. They will feel more connected to your brand and are more likely to remain loyal for a longer time. It is not just about posting something and waiting for people to view it. Use the caption to increase engagement by asking a question or adding a call-to-action. On the Stories tab, hold polls or Q&A sessions. Reply to comments left on your posts and reply to any Direct Messages. Taking time to connect with your customers will pay off in the long run. You can create a community for your customers through forums or chat groups as well. These will give you insight into their needs and wants and build a community around your brand. When users feel connected to your brand, they are also more likely to recommend you to others. You should also try to leave a like or comment on posts from your followers. Increasing engagement time is an important aspect of growing your follower count.

Connect with Influencers

Influencer marketing is important in this day and age. You can invest money in connecting with influencers who create content in line with your brand. If they post content promoting your brand on their account, it will direct their followers to your page. This is an easy way to gain more followers. You don't have to spend a lot on big influencers if your budget is low. Micro-influencers are just as effective in helping brands grow. Find influencers that focus on your niche and will work with you for a reasonable cost. You can help them out by promoting them on your account as well. This way, you can cross-promote each other. Working with influencers also helps to build faith in your company. Their followers already trust in their recommendations, and this makes them trust in your business as well. When influencers post about your brand and talk to their followers about you, it leads to organic growth for your account.

Use Hashtags

Hashtags are an easy way for people to search for content. You can add up to 30 hashtags on every post you upload on Instagram. These hashtags work like keywords used to search for things on search engines, but you should do research on finding the most popular hashtags related to your business and content. Don't use random hashtags that have nothing to do with your brand or your content. If your business is about health and fitness, use hashtags related to that niche. Don't use hashtags that are completely unrelated or irrelevant. Don't use random hashtags like #like or #love. Users will click on your post when they see it on their search results and might even follow your account if they like your content.

You can even try creating a few hashtags that are specific to your brand. Brand-specific hashtags are an easy way to make your brand more searchable. It is also something that other users can use when they buy products from you or just want to mention you on their own post. You can also create hashtags for any contest or promotion you run. It can be among the contest terms to use these hashtags on reposts or stories to qualify. You can also encourage them to use these hashtags on other platforms and do the same across your online presence.

Although you are allowed to use 30 hashtags for your post, it doesn't mean you have to. It is more important to use the right hashtags. Using too many and adding random words will only make your post look like spam. You can also avoid an unattractive caption by using the hashtags in your comment section instead. If you look at the most popular influencers and brands, you will see that they rarely use more than 5-6 hashtags for each post.

Chapter Four: Instagram Ads

What is Instagram Advertising?

Instagram advertising is how you pay for sponsored content to be shown to a larger targeted audience on Instagram. It is used for building brand awareness, increasing website traffic, generating leads, and making conversions. In tune with the platform's overall concept, ads are in the form of images or videos, and not text ads.

Investing in Instagram ads will allow you to run well-rounded campaigns for your business. It is useful at every stage of the funnel, is extremely effective at increasing brand awareness and driving conversions.

Here's why you should invest in Instagram ads:

They are Integrated with Facebook Ads

Facebook advertising has great campaign customization options and diverse formatting. When you invest in Instagram advertising, you also get these benefits since they are fully integrated. The high engagement from Instagram, along with the targeting capabilities of Facebook, will help your campaign be a success.

Ample Engagement Opportunities

The users on Instagram are interested in engaging with brands on the platform. According to statistics, users are 50 times more likely to engage with ads on Instagram than on Facebook, and nearly double that amount again compared to branded content on Twitter.

Ad Recall is Higher on Instagram

It is not just about the higher engagement on Instagram. The ad recall from ads on the platform is nearly three times that from other sites. Users are much more likely to click on the ads and remember them when they view them on Instagram.

You already know that there are millions of users on Instagram. At least 500 million users are active on it every single day. This is reason enough to be on the platform for your own brand as well. It's likely that nearly all, if not all, of your competitors are already there and utilizing the benefits of Instagram marketing. Statistics show that about 53% of users follow their favorite brand accounts on Instagram. Brand engagement is ten times more than on Facebook, 80 times than that on Twitter, and 50 times higher than on Pinterest. This should be enough to convince you to use Instagram ads for your business too!

It is extremely easy to create and run ads on Instagram. Here you will get a step-by-step tutorial on how to do it yourself.

How to Run Ads on Instagram

Step 1: Go to Ad Manager on Facebook

To get started with Instagram advertising, you have to use the Ad Manager on Facebook. Instagram does not have any specific Ad Manager on its platform. From there, you will be taken through levels like Campaign and Ad Set. You can use these to create a single ad set with multiple ads, or a single campaign with multiple ad sets. When you are at the campaign level, you will be choosing the objective for the ad. When you are at the ad set level, you will be deciding on the target audience, schedule, budget, bidding, and placements. Once you are at the ad level, you have to decide on the creative component.

Step 2: Choose an Objective at the Campaign Level

The first thing to do while creating an ad for Instagram is to choose your ad campaign's objective. You will have to choose from the following objectives listed under each heading:

Awareness: Reach, Brand Awareness

Consideration: Engagement, Traffic, App Installs, Messages, Video views, Lead Generation

Conversion: Conversions, Store visits, Catalog sales

- Brand awareness is for showing the ad you create to an audience who might be interested in your brand

- Reach is for showing the ad to as many users on Instagram as possible

- Traffic is for encouraging more visits to your website

- Engagement is for increasing engagement on your posts in the form of comments, likes, event responses, shares, or offer claims

- App Installs will encourage users to download your app

- Video views are for giving priority to increasing views on your videos

- Lead generation will direct users to a lead generation form when they click on the ad

- Messages will encourage users to message your brand for any queries directly

- Conversions will have the goal of generating more conversion like purchases, registrations, or email sign-ups

- Store visits are for businesses that have physical stores at some locations, and this will encourage users to visit the stores

- Catalog sales will display items from the Facebook product catalog of your business to any users who might be interested

You must choose objectives that align with the goals of the ad you are creating. You need to have a clear idea about what you want from the campaign. If you want your video ad to drive conversions, select the conversions objective. If you select the video views objective, it will just increase views for your ad but not focus on generating any actual conversions from the views. Facebook will use the objective you choose to decide the audience that it will display your ads to. This is how the audience for ads is optimized.

Step 3: Make Decisions at the Ad Set Level

After the campaign level, you move to the ad set level. If you use the ad to send traffic to another location, you will be choosing the exact location to drive traffic. It could be to your app, website, or even messenger.

You will then see the offer to drive conversions.

After this, you get options for targeting. You have access to all the great targeting options from Facebook when you create an ad for Instagram. You may target cold as well as warm leads with this.

Users can be targeted based on demographics like:

- Age
- Gender
- Job title
- Parental status
- Education
- Relationship status
- Languages spoken
- Location

Targeting can also be done on the basis of behavior and interests, such as:

- Dog owners
- Diet
- Online shoppers
- Sports and outdoors

When you don't have custom audiences, you can use the connection-targeting feature. With this, you can target people who are or are not connected to your app, page, or events. For instance, if you select the Facebook Pages option under Connections, you can choose from people who like your page, or the friends of users who like your page. You can also exclude people who already like your page and target a new audience instead.

You can create a custom audience to target like:

- A list of email addresses from your customers

- People who visit your website or page in a certain time period

- People who have previously interacted with the content on your Instagram profile or watched your video for a certain amount of time

Once you create a custom audience for your ad, you can create a lookalike audience that will help you reach customers similar to the segmented audience list you have created.

Step 4: Ad Placements

Under Placements, Automatic placements will already be selected by Facebook. You have the opportunity to change these placements if you click on "Edit Placements."

You can choose to use other placements when you are running Instagram Ads on the newsfeed. But if you run ads on Instagram Stories, you cannot select any other placements. If you select the option of desktop-only ads, you cannot run Instagram ads.

When you choose newsfeed ads, you can enable placements like side column ads on Facebook, or messenger ads.

There are several marketers that think that it is easier to run campaigns with only Instagram Ads enabled since formatting might be simpler. This could affect the cost of running the campaign negatively. Instagram ads can be more expensive to run than other Facebook Ad placements.

It might be better to combine placements and keep the average bids low. This helps advertisers to stay on budget and get better results.

Step 5: Budget and Schedule

After placements, you move on to budgeting. You have two options when it comes to the budget for your ad campaign. You can set a lifetime budget or a daily budget.

Choosing the lifetime budget option will allow Facebook to distribute your ad spend over a certain period. This will make sure that you don't spend more than your Instagram marketing budget, even if you schedule incorrectly.

You can schedule dates to start and end your campaign or select the option of running the ad set continuously. When you set an end date for the campaign, you can be assured that it doesn't get forgotten. The end date can always be extended later if you want.

Step 6: Bidding

There is a bidding system for Ads on Instagram and Facebook. This means that you can win the ad placement for your target audience if you are willing to bid more than others. The bid will depend on what you are optimizing your ad for. You may bid for impressions, clicks, landing page views, etc. Manual bidding can allow you to control the amount you spend for the results you want from the ad. You can put a cap on the bid if you know that there is a certain amount that your lead is worth. This will make sure that you don't spend more than you should on the ad.

You have to be careful while using manual bidding as well. If you choose a maximum bid instead of an average bid on your maximum CPA, you might end up losing out on placements. Ads on Instagram usually cost more than ads on other platforms, so having an average bid might help you maintain control of spending. By selecting an average bid, you will allow the expensive ads to be balanced by other placements that cost less. You won't have to do any manual bidding, and Facebook will be bidding on your behalf automatically. The automatic bids are generally good enough.

Step 7: Creatives at the Ad Level

The creative section is the last stage of creating an Instagram Ad. This level is where you decide what your ad will say or how it looks. Since Instagram is a visual platform, this is a very crucial part of the process.

Instagram Ad Formats

You can use four different formats for ads on Instagram.

Single Image Ads

These can be to the point and very clear. If you want an ad for a single product or for a particular service, this is the type of format you can choose. It works especially well for things that have a high amount of visual appeal. For single image ads, you need an image in the ratio of 1.91:1. The recommended size of the image is 1200 x 628pixels. The text should be less than 20% of this image.

Carousel Ads

If you want to display a number of products to your audience, you can choose to use multiple images. This format gives you the chance to elaborate further on what you want to convey to your audience. You are not restricted to a single image for this. You can choose to add images as well as videos to the carousel. Adding a video can make the ad more engaging for users, but anything you upload will have to be square and not rectangular.

Video Ads

Just like Facebook, the video ads on Instagram will run on auto-play. They also don't have sound when they begin playing automatically. By adding closed captions on the video, you can prompt users to click for sound. Since videos allow you to add a narrative to the ad, you should encourage users to listen with sound. The video ads have a limit of sixty seconds. It is best to create video ads at least 15 seconds long, although you can choose any length up to 60 seconds. The files' minimum width has to be 600 pixels, and the maximum size of the file is 4G.

Instagram Stories

This will be further explained in the next section since they are different from regular ads.

Image and Copy Creation

You will have to choose the ad copy and visual components in the last part of the ad. You can select the video or image first, and the copy can then be based around it. You will see that certain text cannot be applied to Instagram Ads.

For instance, the headline section will be visible on Facebook Ads, but it will not show up on Instagram Ads. To check for such things, you must preview the ad in all the different placements before publishing it. This way, you can make sure that the ad looks how you envisioned.

You should also choose the Call-to-Action button here. It will include options like "Send Message" or "Learn More." Select the option that aligns with what you want your audience to do when they view the ad. You should also consider where the users are in the sales funnel when you choose the option. For instance, if you were targeting new customers, it would be better to choose "Learn More" rather than pushing them to "Shop Now."

Step 8: Connect the Instagram Ad Account to Facebook

It is easy and quick to connect the Instagram Ad account with Facebook. In Ad creation, you can choose the Instagram Account and Page under which you want to run the campaigns. The Facebook Page will probably be linked already. If the Instagram account is not linked, you have two choices. You can run the Instagram Ad under the Facebook Page. Otherwise, you can connect the ads manager to the Instagram account. To link the account, you have to click on "Add an Account." This will give you a login screen on which you can sign into the Instagram account you created for your business.

These steps are all you need to run ads on Instagram! It can take some trial and error to find out what works best for your business, so experiment with different ad types, formats, audiences, placements, and budgets. If you feel a little intimidated by Instagram advertising, you can simply choose to Boost Posts.

How to Boost Instagram Posts

Instagram gives you the option to pay and promote a particular post from your Instagram account. When you boost a post, you should see an increase in views, likes, and comments. You can only choose the Boost Post option if the Instagram account is a business profile. This option is not available for personal accounts. When you click on any of your posts, you will see the "Promote" option below the image or video.

Once you select the Promote option, you can choose the objective you have in mind for this post. There are two options here, unlike the various options under advertising:

- Get more profile and website visits. Here you can choose to send users to your Instagram profile or your website. You can choose from CTA buttons like Watch More, Shop Now, Sign Up, Learn More, Book Now, and Contact Us.

- Reach people near an address. This helps you choose the location from which you want to target an audience. You can choose a CTA button prompting Directions or Call Now.

You will need to choose the CTA button for the promoted post and then set your budget. You will also be stating how long you want the post to be promoted. Before you submit the post for promotion, take the chance to preview it and make any changes you might think are necessary.

Monitor Instagram Ads

Instagram Ads can be monitored with the Ads Manager. The dashboard will give you everything that you might need to see in a quick overview. This includes cost per action, relevance score, etc. You will be able to see the reach from your ad, but this number is not as important as you might think. The results from the ad are the main metric you want to focus on.

You need to watch the performance of the ad closely as it runs. Your CPC might increase when the frequency increases, but other metrics may sink. By closely monitoring the campaign, you will understand what is working on the ad and what isn't. Ineffective campaigns can then be paused before they cost more than they are worth. You can then relocate this money for another campaign that performs better and gives you better ROI.

Ads on Instagram Stories

Now let's talk about running ads on Instagram Stories. These are a part of the ad system on Facebook, but they work a bit differently. These ads can only run by themselves and do not work like newsfeed ads. This means that you cannot run these ads with other placements under the same ad set. The creative, as well as technical requirements for Instagram Story Ads, are quite different. You will still be able to use the same options for bidding, targeting, budgeting, and scheduling, but the similarities between newsfeed ads and the ones on the story end there.

Objectives of Ads on Instagram Stories

The placement of your ad on Stories is different from newsfeed ads, and the objectives are different. The following are the objectives you can choose from:

- Reach will focus on showing the ad to a larger number of people

- Video views will allow the ad to be viewed by as many people as possible

- Conversions will help to drive conversions like sales and registrations

- Traffic will focus on sending more traffic to your website

- Lead generation is for opening up a form that will automatically be filled up with as much information of the user as possible

- Mobile app installs will encourage more users to download your app

It is usually better to choose Conversions, Traffic, Mobile App installs, or Lead generation instead of Reach and Video Views. You get the option to add a link to your Story Ad when you choose from the former options. This makes the ad a lot more actionable and will give you better results.

There might be more objectives made available from the story ads with time. When it was first launched, the only objective available was Reach. After choosing the objective you think will benefit your campaign, you can choose the Instagram Story placement.

Technical Requirements for Instagram Story Ads

- Images have to be in the ratio of 9 x 16

- The recommended size for the image is 1080x1920 pixels

- Videos can only be 15 seconds long

- The video has to be of 4:5 vertical aspect ratio

- The minimum width for a video is 600 pixels

- The maximum size of the file is 4 GB

- Videos of the format .mov, .mp4 or .gif are recommended.

The only similarity between story ads and those on newsfeed is that there should be minimum text on the images. If the text is more than 20%, your ad might not be approved.

Another thing to keep in mind is that the aesthetic for Instagram Stories is quite different from newsfeed ads. The features of Instagram stories are similar to Snapchat. You can add stickers, filters, or drawing tools. You should make the ad as fun and attractive as possible with these tools. Although this feature is quite new, it has shown great returns and engagement for brands that have invested in it.

Tips for Instagram Story Ads

Engage the User

It should be something that instantly engages the user and makes them want to watch it. Once the user clicks away from the ad, it is gone and cannot be viewed again. This is why it is important to upload content that will immediately grab the viewer's attention and remain memorable. You can go the humorous route to make the ad attention-grabbing, or you could use attractive textual cues. You can also upload images that will make the user stop for a moment and think.

Upload Videos

Videos are a powerful way to grab attention via Instagram stories. It will give your ad a longer time on their screen, and you also get the chance to elaborate on your point. A story with an image will only be viewed for five seconds, while a video can give you a fifteen-second ad.

Add Your Brand and Logo

Since Stories only give you a short time to make an impression, there should be a clear placement of the brand name and logo. This will make the viewer remember that the ad belongs to your brand and increases brand recognition. Even if they don't click on the link attached to the ad fast enough, they will be able to search for your brand.

Cost of Instagram Ads

Costs are an important factor for any kind of marketing, and this applies to Instagram ads. You probably want to use Instagram ads but are now wondering how much it will cost. Well, there are a lot of factors that will affect the costs for your ads on Instagram.

Estimate the Ad Spend

When the option to advertise on Instagram was first made available, it was instantly noticeable that it cost more than Facebook ads. The CPAs and the CPCs were higher than Facebook Ads despite being under one campaign. The cost of your Instagram Ad can fluctuate at any time. There are many factors like relevance score and the bidding system that affect the cost of the ad. It is important to monitor the ad spend carefully since the cost of current campaigns can also change every day. It is impossible to establish a particular cost per day of an Instagram ad.

According to research:

- The CPC of Instagram Ads consistently increases through the year

- The CPC does not vary much by age

- The highest CPC is from iPhones and then iPads.

When you run an ad, it is important to keep an eye on the relevance score and frequency metrics. When frequency scores get exceedingly high, the actions reduce, which negatively impacts the ad's relevance score over time, but when the relevance score is good, it will allow you to keep the CPC costs low. It is better to invest more money into a campaign with better relevance scores so you can make the most of the ad spend.

Tips for Successful Instagram Ad Campaigns

Since there is a lot of competition on Instagram, you have to make sure that you run an ad optimized for the platform. This will help you get the best results with the best CPC and allow you to make the most out of your ad spend.

Test Various Formats

It is always better to test out every element of the ad. You should try various images, videos, copies, and formats. You can then see what your audience is more responsive to. Testing is the only way to figure out what is best for your business or your audience.

Closed Captions for Videos

As mentioned before, Instagram video ads begin playing without sound. A lot of people continue viewing the ad in silent mode without clicking on it for sound. This means that your audience might not understand what you are trying to convey through the ad. Adding closed captions to videos will allow a better chance of getting through to the viewer and increase retention rates.

Use Images Most Suitable for Instagram

Images used on a Facebook ad or any other social media platform will not necessarily perform well on Instagram. Instagram is a lot more visual, and you need to follow the trends currently popular on the platform. Research has shown that images with single dominant colors, low saturation, bluish tints, and a lot of visual texture tend to do better on the platform. You don't have to follow all these demarcations for your images, but they should give you an idea of what will be better for Instagram ads.

Make Use of the Segmented Lists

Segmented marketing tends to work well on social media platforms. You should try to show products that are relevant to custom audiences. You can create the right messages for your audience from the information you already have on them. You will know what resonates with this segmented audience and thus create the right ad by keeping them in mind.

Focus on the Visuals

Visuals are key on Instagram. You need to upload an image or video that will stand out in the feeds of your viewers. As long as your visuals are great, a simple description for your ad will be enough.

Be Creative

If you want to stand out, get creative with your ads. Doing something unconventional with your ad will help you grab the user's attention. Smart marketing will help you showcase the personality of your brand. Try something different and fun for your Instagram ad to make it stand out among other content.

Hashtags on Instagram Ads

Hashtags are an important part of Instagram, and it is how users can find the content or profiles they are interested in. These hashtags are a core part of the personality of Instagram. You can place hashtags on all your Instagram posts and can even do so on an ad. It is not necessarily the best option to use hashtags on Instagram ads. They might look out of place and too much like spam. If you look at the ads run by other brands, you will notice that they often refrain from adding hashtags to their Instagram Ads since it typically looks better with a great image and concise text.

You also shouldn't use hashtags on your ad because it won't appear on the search results for that hashtag. This happens because they don't work the same way as a regular post. You don't need to rely on hashtags for visibility since you are already paying Instagram for this while the ad is running.

You can add hashtags if the purpose is to add personality to the ads. It should only be done according to copywriting and not for visibility.

You now have enough knowledge to create and run Instagram ads for your brand successfully. Remember that a great deal of trial and error will likely be involved when trying to figure out what ads work best for your business, so don't be discouraged if your ads aren't profitable from the very start. Keep a close eye on the results your ads achieve and tweak them accordingly. Soon enough, you'll have a profitable ad campaign that is targeted perfectly for your desired audience!

Chapter Five: Influencer Marketing

What is an Influencer?

Influencers are people with accounts that have a large and engaged following. They share their opinions and reviews on various products, services, topics, and anything their followers would be interested in. They have established a presence that makes users trust them and follow their recommendations.

Being an influencer is not about having millions of followers. It is more about having a great influence on the people following you. At first, it was all about influencers with the largest following, but people are paying more attention to micro-influencers now. This is because accounts with fewer followers have higher engagement and ROI.

Different Types of Influencers

There are different categories for influencers depending on their following, content, and niche. If you want to invest in influencer marketing, you need to understand what type of influencer is more suitable for your business.

The four major groups of influencers are:

Mega Influencers

Accounts that have more than a million followers are mega influencers. Major public figures or celebrities usually are the owners of these accounts. They usually have an established public presence even before they create an Instagram account. People follow these accounts because it allows them to stay updated with their lives. However, some other accounts build this large following purely from the content they create for Instagram.

Macro Influencers

Accounts that have a following count between 100,000 and 1 million are macro-influencers. These could be famous figures like actors, or micro-influencers who grew their following over time.

Micro-Influencers

Accounts with less than 100,000 followers belong to micro-influencers. These influencers tend to have a specific niche that they create content around. Brands employ their services because of the influence they have in that niche and the high ROI they often provide.

Nano Influencers

Accounts with less than 10,000 followers fall under this category. Although their following is small, they usually have a niche audience and very high engagement. Brands have increasingly been working with these influencers since it is a cost-effective investment that can give better returns than you might expect! Consumers connect better with these influencers and feel that their recommendations are more genuine.

What is Influencer Marketing?

Influencer marketing has different meanings for different people. But the basic meaning of influencer marketing is brands leveraging influencers to drive more traffic to their pages and gain higher conversions. It is a content marketing strategy where a business partners with an influencer to promote their product or service.

Influencer marketing is usually done in the following ways:

- Sponsored posts or stories on Instagram

- Sponsored blog posts

- Sponsored posts on other social media like Facebook or Twitter

- Sponsored events conducted offline hosted by an influencer or where they make an appearance

Businesses use influencer marketing for varied reasons. Certain brands want the influencer to help increase brand awareness, while others are specifically looking for more conversions. Brand awareness is usually one of the primary reasons why businesses pay influencers.

Instagram is the most widely used platform by social media influencers. As they build their influence, they get the opportunity to work with the kind of brands they are most interested in.

Benefits of Influencer Marketing on Instagram

It is Niche Based

There are many ways users can find the niche content they are interested in on Instagram. The easiest way is through hashtags. When influencers use niche specific hashtags, users get instant access to that content. As mentioned, businesses can increase brand awareness by having hashtags specific to their brand or campaign. The Instagram Explore page is the other way users view posts relevant to their interests. Instagram uses its algorithm to constantly provide users with content they are more likely to engage with. This is why influencer marketing is a great way for businesses to increase brand awareness. These influencers have already been tagging their niche, and the business can tap into their follower base.

It is an Organic Approach

Instagram ads are a great tool for promoting your business, but it is a lot more organic to drive traffic through influencer content. Consumers have real-time engagement with influencers on Instagram through features like Instagram Live and Stories. Consumers engage better with influencer content that they relate to as compared to advertisements. Influencers can creatively produce content that can integrate your product seamlessly into the follower's daily life. This way, influencer marketing seems much more like a recommendation from a trusted source, rather than an advertisement from a stranger.

It is Personal

Influencer marketing has been doing better than most other marketing strategies because of the personal connection between influencers and their audience. To succeed with influencer marketing, it is important to leverage a relationship that is genuine and engaging. When a brand employs an influencer as its brand ambassador, its followers trust that the brand is trustworthy as well. They depend on these influencers to tell them about brands that they should or should not buy from. Influencers have already built this relationship, allowing your business to gain from your target audience's relationship with niche influencers. Many brands still don't realize just how engaged followers are with influencer content. This personal approach is rarely possible in any other kind of marketing and is a great opportunity for you to grow your business!

How to Find an Influencer to Support Your Brand

If you want to invest in influencer marketing, you have to know what you should be looking for in an influencer. It is not just about finding someone with the highest follower count.

Here are factors to consider while looking for the right influencer:

Do They Fit Your Brand?

If you are creating an influencer marketing campaign, this is the first thing you need to consider. Find an influencer who creates content that would work for your brand. If your business sells shoes, you shouldn't be working with an influencer whose niche is food. Even if they have millions of followers, those followers are interested in food-related content and not fashion. If you find an influencer in a fashion that fits your brand image, their content would then be more useful for your campaign. A fashion influencer posting about the shoes from your brand would seem more genuine from the consumer's perspective.

To decide if the influencer fits your brand, pay attention to the following:

- The niche that their content falls into.

- The topics that are frequently discussed in their comments and stories.

How High is Their Engagement Rate?

Don't scope out an influencer based on their follower count. The engagement rate metrics are far more important these days. You also need to pay attention to check if the following generated from their content is genuine or fake. If the influencer pays a third party for generating likes and follows, it will do more harm than good to your business. It will also be a waste of your marketing budget since the ROI will be very minimal. By paying attention to the engagement rate, you can find influencers who will really help your brand reach potential customers. When the engagement rate seems in line with the following count, you can work with the influencer. And as mentioned above, nano influencers and micro-influencers often have better engagement rates than larger accounts.

Who Have They Worked with Previously?

Look at the sponsors that the influencer has worked with in the past. Are they businesses that would complement your brand? Are any of them your competitors? Take a look at how their campaigns performed. In doing this, you will get an idea of how your brand's campaign might look on their feed as well.

Do They Communicate Well?

Communication plays an important role in business, and this applies to influencer marketing as well. Pay attention to how a particular influencer communicates with you when you reach out to them. Are they quick to respond? Do they take a lot of time to get back to you or miss deadlines? If there is no clear communication, it will be hard to meet deadlines and content requirements. If you can't rely on them to keep you updated in real-time, it will be difficult for the campaign to run smoothly.

Do They Like Your Brand?

The more authentic the content, the better it is. This is only possible if your influencer really likes your brand. They will put in a genuine effort to promote your business if they love it. If it is just for money, they might not put in much of an effort. Look at their feed and past activity to see if they have previously discussed your brand before the sponsorship. If they have, you can rest assured that they will promote your brand with excitement and creativity.

Influencer Compensation

You have decided to invest in influencer marketing. But how do you compensate them?

Influencers are usually compensated in these three ways:

1. Brands give them free products

2. They are paid up-front

3. They get commissions as affiliates

It depends on the brand and the influencer to decide on a mode of compensation. Different influencers look for different things from a campaign. It also depends on what the brand wants to offer for influencer marketing. Every influencer has a different audience and produces content in a way uniquely suited for their audience. Their performance metrics will also vary.

When brands decide on the compensation for influencers, they consider the following things:

- **Agency Fees:** These usually apply to mega or macro-influencers that work under agencies.

- **Travel Expenses:** If your campaign requires traveling, you will have to consider hotel fees, airline costs, etc. This is an important factor to consider for travel influencers.

- **Production:** The amount of time required for creating the content and what other resources are required.

- **Usage Rights:** Paid media requests, exclusivity requirements, etc.

It is not always easy to decide the type of compensation, campaign, influencer metrics, and deliverables; all have to be considered.

Free Products

With this type of compensation, the brand will provide the influencer with free products or services from their brand. For instance, if a fashion brand wants an influencer to promote their clothes, they could give the clothes to the influencer for free. If a hotel wants a travel influencer to promote their business, they can offer a free stay for the influencer at their hotel. If the influencer likes the products or services from the brand, this might be a good option. Influencers with a small following and minimal impact are quite suitable for such compensation. This can also be used in cases of campaigns like non-profit ones. Influencers working for such campaigns tend to work because they care about a particular cause or like the impact your brand makes.

Paid Compensation

This is monetary compensation made to the influencer for promoting the brand. This is determined by the rates the influencer charges as well as the marketing budget of the brand. Influencers who work full time in this field will usually expect paid compensation since it is their source of livelihood. Those with a large following and high engagement want payment in exchange for their impact on the campaign. Influencers who want paid compensation will usually have predetermined rates and prices.

Affiliate Compensation

This type of compensation involves commissions made via affiliate links. Influencers earn from the clicks and sales made from their unique affiliate links. This type of compensation is usually accompanied by a certain amount of paid compensation as well.

With monetary compensation, you should set an ROI metric. You can set rates accounting to the impressions or reach achieved from the content. Setting a rate helps to control costs and makes the influencer more conscious about your exact expectations from the partnership.

The content medium also plays a role in determining compensation.

- **Instagram Stories:** The cheapest medium to compensate for would be an Instagram story. Since stories are only temporary and require little effort, you don't have to pay as much as you would for a post on their feed. Stories have their own rates, but influencers often offer them as a package deal with other content.

- **Image Posts:** Depending on the influencer's reach, a post could cost you anywhere from a couple of hundred dollars for smaller influencers to thousands of dollars for bigger influencers. Several celebrities collaborating with high-end brands even get a million dollars for posting their content.

• **Video Posts:** Videos will cost you more money since they require a lot more time and effort. Influencers with high engagement will typically charge you a minimum of $500 for each video.

How to Find Influencers

You can find influencers for your marketing campaign in a few different ways:

Through Instagram

You can simply scroll through Instagram by searching for relevant hashtags and look through the accounts of a few influencers. Take a look at their content and engagement and decide if they fit your requirements. If you like their content, you can send them a Direct Message on Instagram or use their personal contact information from the Bio section to reach out to them.

Through Influencer Agencies

These days, a lot of influencers have signed up with agencies that manage their projects. You can reach out to an agency and ask them for recommendations. If you already have an influencer in mind, you can negotiate a contract with the agency. Keep in mind that influencers under agencies usually charge more.

Once you find the right influencer, you can set up a campaign for your brand. After the campaign starts running, you have to evaluate the metrics. It is important to track how the partnership is doing. And it is not just about the number of sales generated. Keep an eye on the following things:

- Study the engagement rate from the campaign

- What sentiment about the brand has the influencer been able to create?

- How much traffic did they generate to your website or other platforms?

- How were the conversions, and what was the revenue generated?

- How many new followers did you get from the influencer marketing campaign?

Evaluate all these factors to understand if you got a decent ROI. You should also take time to evaluate the relationship developed between the brand and the influencer during the campaign. Were they good communicators? Did they deliver on time? Did they follow all the requirements mentioned by the brand? Did the influencer try their best to promote the brand? Did they make an effort to improve on the campaign with their personal input? If the influencer builds a good relationship with your brand, you should try to nurture this for future projects as well. If they don't deliver well, it would be better to look for someone more appropriate for the next campaign.

The concept of influence is not a new one. People have always been influenced by those they admire. For instance, if the popular girl in high school wore something, soon it would be what others are wearing as well. Similarly, people follow what influencers on Instagram do. The concept of influencer marketing has been highly beneficial for eCommerce. Influencers come in all shapes and sizes with all kinds of content in different niches. It could be a mom influencer sharing her recommendations for baby products. It could be a fashion influencer promoting a new brand of clothes. It could be a fitness influencer who makes you want to get up and go for a run every morning. Instagram also allows you to get an inside peek into the lives of celebrities or other public figures who previously seemed out of reach. Brands can utilize the influence that all these people have on the general audience to grow their business to new heights.

Conclusion

Instagram marketing is a lot easier than you might think. As long as you have a strategy in place and follow a step-by-step approach, you can use the platform to your advantage. There is great potential for growth once you start building your brand on Instagram. It is a lot more convenient than traditional marketing methods and a lot more effective as well.

The first step is to sign up and create a business account for your brand. Start posting pictures and use the tips given in this book to work from there. Keep your content flowing with your target audience in mind. Test out different types of advertising, and perhaps give influencer marketing a go!

With the tips provided in this book, you have all you need to grow your business and brand on the Instagram platform. Remember to be patient, test different types of content, tweak your ad campaigns to suit your target audience, and be diligent when deciding which influencers to work with. If you can do all of that, results will undoubtedly follow!

www.ingramcontent.com/pod-product-compliance
Lightning Source LLC
LaVergne TN
LVHW011738060526
838200LV00051B/3221